Ideas
for
CHANGE

Campaign principles that shift the world

2018

Ideas for Change

Campaign principles that shift the world

First published 2018
2. Edition

All illustraions in this book is under Creative Commons Licenses and the book is published under Creative Commons License.

Irene Publishing, Sparsnäs 1010, 66891 Ed, Sweden

E-Mail: irene.publishing@gmail.com

www.irenepublishing.com

Partner for this project:

www.civilengagement.org/

Renewable Freedom
Foundation

This booklet is supported by the Digital Rights Fund of the Renewable Freedom Foundation

ISBN 978-91-88061-29-4

9 789188 061294

90000

Content

"Never doubt that a small group of thoughtful, committed citizens can change the world; indeed, it's the only thing that ever has."

Margaret Mead

Project background and acknowledgements

Ideas for Change is an independent project to help improve the effectiveness of citizen activism. It's a 'tool kit' of around one hundred strategic principles and campaign tactics that - across the centuries - have changed the world for the better.

The project builds on the influential *Rules for Radicals*, created more than forty years ago by pioneering US rights campaigner Saul Alinsky.[1] It updates and expands those principles for the modern era. Although Alinsky's rules set out the basis of grassroots community activism, some of those concepts have become less relevant to present day campaigning. A few have even become risky and counterproductive for some forms of activism.

Ideas for Change emerged from the arenas of information rights and privacy, but its principles should benefit any aspect of direct action. If you look closely at the most successful privacy campaigns of the past forty years, you'll see a clear reflection of the most celebrated actions of the peace movement, consumer rights and environmental activism. The principles of strategy are immutable.

The project started life in 2013 and since then has been enriched by input from hundreds of campaigners, academics and activists who participated in meetings in London, Geneva, Amsterdam, Vienna, Brussels, Sparsnäs (Sweden), Goteborg, Berlin, Rome and Copenhagen.

1   http://en.wikipedia.org/wiki/Rules_for_Radicals

An outline of this work was first unveiled at the Computers, Privacy & Data Protection conference in Brussels in January 2014 and was then tested at a public meeting in Copenhagen the following month. A further meeting hosted by the University of Amsterdam launched and evaluated the first set of draft principles.

I would like to extend my deepest gratitude to the Institute for Information Law at the University of Amsterdam, LSTS at the Vrije Universiteit Brussel, Code Red, Amnesty International, Bits of Freedom (NL), Gus Hosein of Privacy International and Jørgen Johansen and Majken Sørensen from the Nordic Nonviolence Study Group (Sweden) for their invaluable help in supporting and improving this work.

Simon Davies

The project was initiated by Simon Davies and the Code Red initiative and is now administered by the Nordic Nonviolence Study Group (NORNONS), Sparsnäs 1010, 66891 Ed, Sweden (NORNONS is a registered non-profit organisation in Sweden, number 802460-7239)

Welcome!

This resource will help you successfully challenge power and authority.

Whether it's local officials trampling on your rights or a national government destroying our dwindling freedoms, there is a need - and a responsibility - to confront such power. Intrusive bureaucrats, bullying corporations and intemperate lawmakers all need to be reminded that authority requires a respect for dignity and rights. Empowered citizens help ensure that this reminder is never far from their consciousness.

Sometimes we can influence change in a gentle and conventional way, but there are times when the only message is one that's more relentless and even disruptive. That's often the way the world is changed for the better. This text aims to explore all possible options.

In short, this is an activist's armoury. It brings together the wisdom of hundreds of campaigners throughout the centuries to provide a strategic shop-front that lays out campaigning techniques from gentle moral persuasion, to potent non-aggressive power strategies.

The purpose is to equip all campaigners - and particularly those involved in protecting civil rights, consumer rights, privacy and freedoms - with a step-by step guide to enable effective, responsive and confident activism. It sets out principles that will guide decision-making and management.

Some of these ideas are self evident. Some may be counter-intuitive. The aim isn't to create a long thesis out of these concepts, but to itemise them in a bullet-form in a way that might trigger the imagination.

No-one can tell you what's wrong or right - and this text certainly cannot advise on the ethical justification for various campaign tactics. That's a decision you must make for yourself. But for reasonable people in any vaguely civilised environment, there is one rule that applies to all situations: campaigners should never hurt people or endanger life. Beyond that, almost any action can be morally justified. And when I say "any action", this historically includes criminal damage, sabotage, disruption, law-breaking, circumvention, whistleblowing, interference, systematic irritation and institutional subversion. You decide. It's reasonable to argue that if governments do it... so can you!

You will notice an emphasis on the principles of campaign structure and management. In my experience, these aspects are just as crucial as strategy and tactics. Those principles may not be so exciting to implement, but they will certainly create the bedrock for resilient and shock-resistant campaigns.

Introduction

Nestled in the heart of the Yorkshire moors in the North of England is a secret that the British government has been trying to keep under wraps for more than half a century.

Among the peaceful cow fields stands a stark metallic eyesore that sprawls across a square mile. The world's biggest electronic spy station - the Menwith Hill base - hosts a giant complex of computers and radomes that monitor the communications of a third of the world (a raydome is a circus tent-style protective shield for radar and interception equipment).[1] Although it's located on British soil, the base is occupied and controlled by American authorities – most notably the National Security Agency (NSA), made infamous in recent times by the whistleblower Edward Snowden.

To some people, the existence of this base in an obscenity. Protests are regularly staged outside (and sometimes – spectacularly - even inside) its gates. But there's one campaigner in particular who has been a dogged and persistent activist there for more than two decades, providing a constant public reminder that the individual can make a difference.

Lindis Percy[2], a now-retired nurse, midwife and health visitor from the nearby town of Harrogate, decided to make a stand against the Menwith Hill base at a time when few people had even heard of the NSA or its now infamous global communications

---

1 http://www.raf.mod.uk/organisation/rafmenwithhill.cfm
2 http://en.wikipedia.org/wiki/Lindis_Percy

spy network. She stalked the base year after year, inviting prosecution.

Fifteen prison sentences and nearly five hundred arrests later, Lindis became a catalyst for public awareness of the base and what it represents. With tenacious colleagues from the Campaign for the Accountability of American Bases (CAAB) she not only humbled the defence authorities, but she also succeeded in highlighting the hypocrisy and unfairness of laws that protect powerful overseas interests at the expense of the rights of British citizens.

Throughout history, remarkable people like Lindis Percy have inspired societies to peacefully challenge authority. To achieve this end they have looked across military and political history to discover keys that can unlock social reform - the triggers to create mass movement of thought and action. Most important of all, such people consistently prove that a combination of astute tactics, collaboration, persistence and a deep respect for truth and ethics can make a real difference – regardless of the odds.

The spark that challenges regressive power can be found in even the smallest and most controlled communities, urging us to work together to achieve a greater vision. You will see this spirit embodied in countless campaigns that strive to reform corrupt authority and bad practice.

Hidden behind most of these movements of thought there's at least one strategic blueprint for action. It is an essential element. In most cases, a belief - no matter how powerful or inspiring - does not magically turn into a movement. And a movement does not naturally shift human thought and behaviour. Laying out the enabling strategies will help all campaigns to become more successful.

In spite of the good intentions that inspire them, most campaigns do not survive long enough to achieve even a partial victory. Many die at an early stage through lack of direction or sustenance. This mortality rate improves when campaigners gain a clearer understanding of the opportunities and options open to them. For societies to change for the better, the odds of campaign survival need to improve. Cataloguing specific campaign strategies helps build a stronger narrative between activists. It also accelerates collaboration on campaign development.

The need for direct action to protect human rights and freedoms is as pressing now as in any time in recent history. Privacy and freedom of expression are assaulted daily by new forms of control and censorship. Meanwhile, the idea of individual autonomy is becoming more theoretical. Freedom of movement, association and speech are increasingly subject to the constraints of license, as governments quietly build a regime of control that – in many nations - is closed and unaccountable.

The geopolitical realm is starkly shifting. Britain voted to leave the EU. Countries across Europe have become defensive and nationalistic. And then of course, there is the rise of the Trump presidency in the US. The stakes are high, and to prevent a dire outcome, citizens must take action that is effective, potent and at times combative. Such is the history of democracy and freedom. Actions to protect rights must be more influential than the tactics of fear that take those rights away.

None of this should indicate a challenge to the Rule of Law. As one Canadian legal analysis explained "A recognition that civil disobedience can play a healthy role in Canadian society does not undermine the rule of law. Quite the reverse, actually. For the citizens of a country to respect law, their legal and governmental systems must, on the whole, seem legitimate to them. When a law is so offensive to the conscience of a significant number of people that they are willing to engage in or support the breaking of that law, then society as a whole is put on notice that change may well be needed."[3] Civil disobedience has been used to advance some of the most pressing public policy issues of the day – for example, the right of women to vote, desegregation of the American South and the need to end Apartheid in South Africa.[4]

A brief primer on campaigning (particularly for newbies)

Some of you are reading this resource because you're angry and frustrated about an issue that matters to you. You intend making a difference. Somewhere, there's an enemy and a target - even if you haven't yet figured out exactly what the target is. But one way or the other, you plan to confront the problem head-on.

Presumably, your aim is to challenge authority. You may imagine a confrontation with corporations or with government - their rules or their plans.

---

3   http://en.wikipedia.org/wiki/Lindis_Percy
4   ibid

Your goal may be to remove a bad government scheme - or even a bad government. Whatever the issue, it makes sense to take a deep breath and look around to see how other people have tackled similar challenges. That awareness will help identify the most effective and relevant strategies. Ideas for Change argues for an ethical approach to whatever action you decide on, but it doesn't take sides - and it certainly doesn't advise against more blatant measures such as lawbreaking or civil disobedience.

Of course, some of you are seasoned campaigners. You will be accustomed to the measured energy that's often needed to prevent burnout over a long term campaign. For those who are new to campaigning and activism, you're probably feeling charged up, whether through fury, indignation or a longing for retribution.

Friends may cruelly say you've become a little obsessed. Proceed regardless. Obsession is merely a term used by disinterested onlookers to characterise highly driven reformers. It's only when 'obsession' turns into neurosis and paranoia that your goals may be fatally compromised.

If you've already identified an enemy and a target, you may need to reassess. Sometimes the enemy and the target aren't quite what you expect. Ask any military leader. Disabling a bakery may have more value than sinking ten ships. And just because someone wears the uniform of the enemy, that doesn't make them the best target. Focusing (for example) on a highly visible underling in local government is one approach, but a more appropriate adversary may be the senior central department official who signed the administrative order or budget approval. More likely, the true enemy is the invisible policy adviser who created the political environment that made the whole mess possible.

During the bitter battle over the UK national identity card in the early 2000's, the campaign group NO2ID decided that instead of focusing all firepower on government ministers responsible for the ID policy, attention should be drawn to the traditionally invisible bureaucrat who was making the scheme possible.[5]

As a wealthy consultant seconded to the government to manage the identity card proposals, James Hall - together with his castle-like home - could easily be portrayed as a co-enemy. The more pressure that was placed on Hall, the more ministers felt uncomfortable publicly identifying with him.

A word of caution however. Be fuelled by your emotions, but don't let them lead you into false optimism or a worthless action. Think of yourself as a cold strategist and look at the entire spectrum of possibilities before making a choice.

Whether you identify as a moderate reformer or a hard-line militant has relevance to the strategies you'll decide on. Strategies and tactics are tools for everyone, but any good strategist of whatever genre needs to know the supreme importance of commitment, staying power, the popularity of your cause and whether you can be realistic in your campaign management.

---

5 http://www.morningadvertiser.co.uk/General-News/Government-misled-over-national-ID-cards

Militant, reformer, activist or advocate?

Radical action is far more popular than most people imagine. There are very few people who can go through life without challenging authority in one way or another. Even those who appear submissive by nature have probably taken a stand. At a certain moment, even the most anally-retentive conformist will resist forces that threaten a quiet life.

We were influenced in childhood by an empire of films, plays, books, philosophies, ideologies and folklore, all celebrating the lives and legend of law-breaking individuals who took hold of powerful ideas and - against great odds - influenced and improved the world. They tell us that much of what we cherish - including our rights and freedoms - was made possible because of the maverick activist. Sadly, in the adult mind, those important lessons often degenerate into fairy tales.

It's all too often the case that 'other' people's crusades are viewed even by friends and family as selfish and pointless. It's not surprising therefore that people who do something radical are often portrayed so poorly. This, of course, is as disheartening as it is unfair. The stereotype of the radical as a corrosive, left-leaning obsessive is far from the truth. In reality people who take radical action are found right across the human spectrum - and often in the most surprising forms.

Standing up to authority is one of the defining processes of a healthy mind. Taking steps to challenge regressive or unfair power is a natural response for any reasonable self respecting member of society. Indeed through the course of human history, every step forward required a brave challenge to rules and conventions. The great movements that shaped society were made possible because a mass of people supported a radical idea and abandoned the way things used to be done.

To defy unfair power doesn't make you "a" radical or "an" activist, it just means you took action to protect something you believe in. The radical stereotype is a convenient way for entrenched power to devalue those who seek to reform bad practices. Doing something radical does not define you; it enhances you.

Of course there's a stereotype to conveniently fit any campaigner. It is said the advocate wears a suit and advances his quite reasonable cause through reasoned argument. The campaigner sold his suit on eBay and presses his dubious cause through protest. The activist wears his father's suit to court and pushes his unreasonable cause through aggressive action. And so on.

It's impossible to accurately profile the radical. Consider the gentle great grandmother who caused hell for her local council for months by standing on a busy street corner every day with a placard that read "City hall thieves... give my house back" . Or others who occupied a rubbish dump outside Manila and turned it into their town, defying military and police efforts to remove them.[6] Perhaps closer to home, a family who stood by their father as he militantly defied his employer over discrimination - and watched helpless as the bank took away their home.

---

6   http://www.independent.co.uk/news/world/one-dies-as-police-clear-manila-dump-1584053.html

Thankfully, in all those examples, the underdog eventually won, though victory is often at the end of a long and painful road. How you define such people depends on how you resonate with them.

Contrary to popular imagination, most people become activists not by attending a local meeting of radicals, but through day-to-day life experience. The spark might be mismanagement of a shopping centre or a sudden awakening that it's wrong for the police to collect DNA from everyone in an entire area. Some people become activists because their children came home from a camping trip with industrial waste on their clothes, and others because they lost their job in a multinational takeover.

These are people who could best be described as ordinary folk with extraordinary beliefs. They are characterized by institutions as subversive, but are more often what one judge in a recent UK trespass case over environmental activism described as "decent men and women with a genuine concern for others" who "acted with the highest possible motives".[7]

Sadly, for many people, the instinct to act radically is subdued by powerful influences from childhood. Those influences set a default acceptance of authority that can be shifted only by exceptional circumstances.

In the reform activity that you might call "action for change" there are seven main labels for the challengers. These, in order of severity, are: advocate, reformer, campaigner, activist, radical, militant and extremist. In reality, the activities of each of them intersect, but the general social image of each is clearly defined and the stereotypes are fixed.

---

7   https://insideclimatenews.org/print/6892?page=2

How you're labelled often depends on the person labelling you. If you were campaigning for better work conditions, your employer would almost certainly affix a less endearing label than the one your workmates would choose, (though sadly, that isn't always the case).

In the end, it barely matters how you are categorised or by whom. The integrity of your beliefs and the outcome of your actions will define you.

General notes on strategy v. tactics

Campaigners, understandably, can become uncertain about the difference between strategy and tactics.

In short, strategy is the overall game plan to an outcome, while tactics are the individual techniques used within that plan. A political election strategy may involve hundreds of tactics set within an overall blueprint with a single strategic objective.

Sun Tzu expresses the difference in the words "Strategy without tactics is the slowest route to victory; tactics without strategy is the noise before defeat". Most new campaigns start with a discussion of tactics - and that's where they often end. Tactics are fun; strategy can be hard work.

Strategy is critically important, particularly in the early stages of any campaign. It's your reference point, your blueprint and your anchor line. Any action you take may trigger a spectrum of adverse consequences. A solid strategy anticipates such risks.

This doesn't mean strategies should be static. Indeed, campaigns often disintegrate because they fail to see alternative strategies. Like nations, campaigners can develop a fixed view of the world and then become institutionally blind to new opportunities and risks. Campaigns also fail because their leaders affix their ego to a preconceived way of doing things.

The processes for any successful campaign can be counter intuitive. Strategy is a living and responsive integrated stream of reasoning and imagination, rather than a set of static equations.

True, the object of good strategy is to win, but the classic approach of aggressive combat is only one possible approach. The first rule of strategy reminds us that the justification for battle is not self-evident; it must be proved. There are times for battle and there are times when doing nothing can be the most effective tactic of all. Open conflict of any kind can hand the opponent a fatal advantage. That approach should never be pursued unless the strategic or symbolic basis is overwhelmingly in your favour.

A good strategist never decides the nature of engagement until all the options have been considered. Cementing a strategy before calculating both its risk and its benefit to the opponent will create an uncertain outcome. Almost any action you take will involve risk. For example (adopting a military maxim), a functional force fighting a dysfunctional force is best just to lie in wait. An agile and adaptive force needs to do little other than play mind games against a monolithic force. Think... Vietnam War.

In acting this way, an informed and empowered new generation of rights advocates is making a real difference. However (considering for just a moment the converse of the above), those campaigners are stretched thin and are often - perhaps advisedly - required to adopt genteel and conventional strategies, even if they miss opportunities for more successful aggressive action.

Intelligent stories from military history tell us precisely how technology and strategy fail, why the effect of politics and law are often illusory and the sometimes infinitely random consequence of strategy. However they also tell us about the nature of chaos caused by unexpected grit in the machine. Becoming grit in the machine is sometimes all that campaigners can hope for: an unanticipated, unwelcome and disruptive irritant. This is often a valuable achievement in its own right – indeed it's the grit that creates the pearl.

The need for smart and effective activism is as great now as ever before, particularly in fields characterized by highly complex technology and law. Apart from notable exceptions - often triggered by political transition - powerful institutions are resistant to all but symbolic change. Many people who control such entities have disdain for the public voice and seek out PR advisers who confirm this negativity.

For example, the trend for companies to develop Corporate Social Responsibility policies has shifted in many cases toward a public relations exercise[8] while corporate spending

---

8 The arguments against CSR, Corporatewatch, http://www.corporatewatch.org/?lid=2688

on political lobbying in the US has more than doubled since 1998.[9] Corporate lobbying in Europe remains a largely opaque and unregulated activity.[10]

Lobbying for legal and regulatory change in the favour of large organizations is now a complex industry in its own right. Meanwhile, the institutional consumer protections such as regulators and watchdogs are frequently becoming more timid and less effective. And, of course, corruption, secrecy, intrusion and denial of rights have become part of the institutional DNA of many countries.[11] Little wonder then that there is need for more effective activism.

Given the task required to challenge such dysfunction, this publication argues the case for a resurgence of more empowered activism and more potent strategies aimed at destabilization and disruption of regressive institutions and ideas.

The arguments in favour of ethical conflict are not unique or even unusual. They borrow from countless sources and are embraced to varying degrees by many activists and reformers. The packaging can vary, but the principles are ancient.

In 2015 I had the pleasure of spending a couple of days with Rick Falkvinge, founder of the Swedish Pirate Party. Rick gave me a copy of his 2014 book "Swarmwise: the tactical manual to changing the world". I had never read this book. I had

---

9 Centre for Responsive Politics http://www.opensecrets.org/lobby/
10 Corporate Europe Observatory http://www.corporateeurope.org/pressreleases/2011/lobby-millions-missing-transparency-register-alter-eu-campaigners-say
11 Transparency International Global Corruption Barometer 2010 http://www.transparency.org/policy_research/surveys_indices/gcb/2010

never before met Rick. And yet the principles he laid out in Swarmwise resonate so closely with Ideas for Change that I no longer have any doubt that the principles of campaigning are indeed universal. The challenge we address in these pages is how to make those principles real and viable for everyone

The principles

General principles of influence

1. Focus on the 'Big Five' emotional triggers: hypocrisy, unfairness, deception, secrecy and betrayal. Many campaigns succeed because they focus on underlying factors that trigger the public psyche. Time and time again, the deceit and hypocrisy of authorities emerge as common lightning rods for public anger. Making these the bedrock of a campaign will magnify the chances of success.[1]

2. A truly influential campaign will not only disrupt bad initiatives, it will also shift underlying beliefs. Bad policies often stem from beliefs and fears that are misplaced or ill informed. Building an effective framework creates immunity against future destructive initiatives.

---

1 The successful campaign against the Anti Counterfeiting Trade Agreement (ACTA) in Europe reflected some on these core drivers for public support, particularly secrecy, unfairness and deception http://techpresident.com/news/22311/germany-activists-help-coordinate-europe-wide-anti-acta-protests

3.

Your size isn't as significant as how you use it. Some of the most influential agents of change are small operations working on the basis of ingenuity, simplicity and flexibility. Many of these players exhibit characteristics that define them as militaristic strategists.[2]

---

2 Margaret Mead expressed this dynamic as: "Never doubt that a small group of thoughtful, committed citizens can change the world; indeed, it's the only thing that ever has." Consider, for example, the work of Rosa Parkes, who together with a small band of strategically-minded supporters, changed the face of US civil rights for all time.

4. **The lone maverick can have more punching power than large institutions.** Following the principle of "size doesn't matter", a single individual has the advantage over even the biggest campaigning organisations. Media love a 'David and Goliath' scenario, while governments and corporations struggle with the concept of fighting flesh and blood rather than an entity.[3]

---

3 Austrian student Max Schrems http://europe-v-facebook.org/EN/en.html for example. has been deified by media over his struggle to bring Facebook to account over its data practices. And even though Schrems has many supporters, the press continues to promote him as a lone maverick, a situation that the social media giant cannot easily grapple with. In a similar vein, US privacy campaigner Katherine Albrecht almost single-handedly traumatised the American retail sector over its covert use of RFID "spy" technology, and forced industry-wide reform through astute strategy. http://www.spychips.com/katherine-albrecht.html

The Privacy Surgeon: "Why we should all celebrate the maverick activist" http://www.privacysurgeon.org/blog/incision/weekend-reflection-why-we-should-all-celebrate-the-maverick-activist/

5. **Don't pretend to be what you're not.** It used to be, several decades ago, that campaigners could use the principle "Power is not only what you have, but what your opponent imagines you have". That is no longer the case. Web analytics tools and search engines allow your opponents to easily identify your true influence and support. If you are a small and under resourced outfit, admit it. There are huge advantages.[4]

---

4 Privacy International, for example, shifted the global privacy environment throughout the 1990's quite openly with only two staff who were equipped with little more than a ruthless strategic tenacity.

6. **Play on your opponents fears.** Perception of the scale of a threat from a campaign, whether real or imagined, can be magnified through the cautious (and plausibly deniable) use of disinformation.[5]

7. **The bigger they come, the harder they fall.** The more powerful and better known your opponent, the higher the stakes. Contesting such an opponent has immediate political and media currency and attracts support from the opposition's existing combatants. The right action against a big name, say the NSA or Google, will cause waves. You need to find a claim, an injustice, a danger - and then frame it in a surprising way. Media will take notice.

---

5   This principle was highlighted to great effect when Saul Alinsky threatened to occupy all the toilets at Chicago's O'Hare airport unless the Mayor addressed the housing issue for poor people. The Major, aware that there was no legal basis to stop the activist, caved in rather than risk a potential international embarrassment. Again reflecting on Privacy International's experience, a 72-hour campaign bringing together publicly trusted figures who opposed the government's plan to link all major computer systems, utterly undermined confidence in the scheme and forced its abandonment in days over the fear that an avalanche of high-profile opponents would follow. The reality was that the opposing voices had already been exhausted.

https://www.privacyinternational.org/node/309

Principles of conduct and integrity

8. **Be scrupulous with the truth.** Never lie or yield to the temptation of making stuff up. A group claiming to represent the public interest does itself - and the public - a disservice by manipulating the truth. The long-term credibility damage can be substantial. Be passionate, but stick to the facts.

9. **Check your facts until it hurts.** Fact checking is critically important as even the smallest error can be magnified and leveraged by your opponents.[6]

10. **Develop a profile of quiet confidence.** Particularly at the early stage of a campaign, when you're trying to win over an ambivalent audience, try to avoid being shrill or dogmatic. Maintain your rage but focus on facts and arguments rather than loud rhetoric. A group that can look confident without being brash - or win and not go over the top - will carry more support. As with any public speaking engagement, strive to get your audience to resonate with your message before turning up the heat.

---

6   For example, the influential London School of Economics analysis of the UK national identity card scheme, which was credited with creating the foundation for the demise of the scheme, was almost fatally compromised because it inadvertently cited "retina scan" instead of "iris scan", an oversight that was then relentlessly exploited against the report both by the inventor of the iris algorithm and by the government.

11.
The strength of your argument depends on the integrity of your commentary. Unless you are strategically playing to extremes, make sure your commentary is engaging and polemic, but grounded in reality. Saying the Home Secretary is like Hitler may get a giggle in some quarters, but half the listeners will instantly dump you – even if he does resemble Hitler. Saying that the Home Secretary's plans are *similar* to those Hitler forced through in 1939 is more likely to win you support.

12.
Lawbreaking must rest on a solid ethical foundation. Sometimes, law breaking is justified – even necessary - but if you intend breaking the law, find the moral basis. Look for judgments that question that law, read parliamentary debate and be very visible. Don't waste yourself serving time invisibly in prison. A carefully researched act of law breaking resting on solid ethical grounds can be potent for a campaign.[7]

---

7 For example, in 1996 four women peace activists entered a British Aerospace hangar and – using domestic hammers - disabled a Hawk jet that was about to be sent to Indonesia, where it would have caused the deaths of innocent East Timorese people. In the trial that followed, the women successfully argued that undertaking the 'criminal damage' was a duty rather than a crime. They were in fact acting to prevent a crime of greater magnitude. All were acquitted. http://www.monbiot.com/1996/07/30/hawks-and-doves/ Be aware though that in many countries there is no guarantee of a jury system.

13. **Never make a threat you aren't prepared - or aren't able - to follow through.** It's bad practice to do so. You might get away with it one time in three, but you'll soon get a "the sky is falling" reputation if you persist.

14. **Never breach your own ethos.** This is a key risk area that would allow an opponent to play the hypocrisy card, which can be highly damaging. Make sure all volunteers and staff are regularly informed about possible areas of risk and that they know the principle and practices of the campaign. Scrupulously observe the standard you demand of your opponent.

Guiding strategic principles

15. **Robust activism is driven by goals, excited by tactics and calmly guided by strategy.** Campaigners should never fall into the trap of confusing strategy with ingenious tactics. Tactical initiatives can be crucial for raising awareness and sensitivity on a subject, but they may be ineffective in the longer term is they are not connected to an integrated strategy.

16. **Conflict is not always the best strategy.** There are times for battle, and there are times when doing nothing can be the most effective tactic of all. Open conflict of any kind can hand the opponent an advantage. Such an approach should never be pursued unless the strategic or symbolic basis is overwhelmingly in your favour.

17. Risk-assess your strategy to anticipate turbulence. The art of campaigning imagines an elegant victory, but the science of campaigning devises a robust, shock resistant bus for the journey. Be a bus! Build risk mitigation into your strategic framework. Anticipate turbulence and disappointment.

18. Never decide the nature of engagement with an opponent until you've looked at all the options. Deciding a strategy before calculating both its risk and its benefit will create an uncertain outcome. Almost any action you will take involves risk. For example (adopting a military maxim), a functional force fighting a dysfunctional force is best just to lay in wait. An agile and adaptive force needs to do little other than play mind games against a monolithic force. Think... Vietnam War.

19. Never assume that the target of your campaign is actually the right target. Sometimes your imagined enemies aren't the best target. Ask any military leader: sometimes disabling a bakery has more value than sinking ten ships. And just because someone wears the uniform of the enemy, that doesn't make them the most worthy target. Shooting at a back-office underling in local government is one tactic, but the more worthy enemy may be the senior official who signed the administrative order or budget approval. More likely, the true enemy is the invisible policy adviser who created the political environment. Conduct thorough research.

20. Whenever possible, go outside the expertise of your **opponent.** This is a crucial principle. It involves drawing the opposition out (for example at public meetings) to deal with questions that they are incapable of answering. Given the moral authority that large organizations attempt to assert, inability to engage broad issues of social concern does not reflect well.

LONG LIVE RESISTANCE AUNTIE! SYK.

21. Make the opponent live up to its own book of rules. Government in developed nations is a soft target here, given the extent of internal and external rules that are publicly available. Being signatory to an international convention, for example, provides opportunities to assert hypocrisy. Companies are also vulnerable due to their published environmental, CSR or community partnership policies. Find the contradictions and then hammer then as loudly and as often as you can.

22. A campaign won in the blink of an eye can be lost in a heartbeat. With rare exceptions, campaigns that achieve their objectives tactically without winning the hearts and minds of all stakeholders tend to be Pyrrhic and can become redundant with the first high-profile media scare story that challenges your position.[8]

---

8   The massive 1987 national campaign against the Australian national identity card – possibly the biggest rights campaign in the country's history – overturned the scheme in a mere fourteen weeks, but this was not a long-enough period of public exposure of the issues to prevent the government introducing the even more intrusive Tax File Number scheme the following year.

23. There is rarely an outright victory, only an outright shift. It's important to understand the difference between disrupting a project and destabilizing a broad agenda.[9]

---

9   For example, European privacy regulators have consistently swatted Google over its poor data protection practices. Initially confident that the advertising giant has been humbled into complying with EU law, they later discovered that the company had outflanked them with new and more aggressive data practices. http://www.out-law.com/articles/2014/january/google-served-maximum-fine-by-french-data-protection-authority-over-privacy-policy-failings/ Many regulators now recognise that there has been no outright victory over the company's illegal practices, only a shift in public perception. No campaigner or reformer should ever assume outright victory on any issue.

24. Any criticism by a major opponent can become an endorsement for your campaign.

Even the slightest reference to a campaigner by a government or corporation should be seen as the jewel in the campaigning crown. Such a reference can be exploited in numerous ways to create the impression of intimidation or bullying. More importantly, it gives you credibility. Any attempt by the opposition to intimidate, bully or persecute can be used as ammunition and possibly win over the public. If the incident is pressed often enough it will become the trigger.[10]

25. When big organizations respond in frustration, they usually fail.

One aim for every serious campaigner should be to goad and intimidate a big opponent to the point where they "lose it". In reality this means goading one small part of the organisation.[11]

26. Engage people at every opportunity.

The public is a time consuming body to deal with, but they're also potentially the richest resource you have. Brainstorm to work out how to reach them and how to best engage them. People can give you stories that are crucial to your campaign.

---

10 British Prime Minister Tony Blair was well aware of this principle. In criticising opponents, he would rarely use their name – just "he" or "she".

11 When Privacy International repeatedly accused Google of "criminal intent" over its interception of private WiFi content as part of its Street View operation, the organisation went off the rails, calling private press briefings, making ad hominem attacks and losing its usually cautious PR balance. http://www.theregister.co.uk/2007/06/11/google_privacy_international/

27. Use the legal system, but with caution.

Legal action is one of the true bottom lines of activism and is an approach that will find common cause with many people. If you're working in a cutting edge field like privacy, remember that law firms will be prepared to consider taking on cases on a pro bono or no win no fee basis, particularly if the issues are unusual or could enhance the companies' reputation. Many well known (and even lesser known) NGOs have law firms at their disposal for this purpose. Self-representation in court is also a possibility in some countries. Consider also, even without free legal help, the potential value of exploiting legal avenues such as injunctions. You'd need to be wary of the cost implications but these can be a low risk, high gain strategy. Just be careful not to put all your eggs in the one legal basket. If you define the integrity of your argument on a strictly legal basis, you may be hostage to fortune over non-legal aspects.

28.
Create dilemma actions against your opponent. Particularly when resources are scarce and pressure is great, adopt the tactics and actions that provide a guaranteed result. Such situations occur when an action is beneficial regardless of its outcome. Writing a letter to a head of government will result in either a celebration of progress, new information, a nil response or a negative. Whichever way, a news peg is created. Likewise, a complaint to a regulator, regardless of win or loss, results in either more information or an opportunity to attack the competence of the regulator.[12]

29.
Know your opponent and know their past. This of course is a game anyone can play, and they do play it. Check public records. Find out how the target is structured and how it functions. Who does what? Where's the funding? Find anything that will give you an edge.[13]

30.
Follow the money. Find specific relationships with banks, vendors and investors. Also, asking questions about unknown monetary relationships is a very potent device.[14]

---

12   The flotilla of boats that set sail in support of the Palestinian cause created a huge dilemma for the Israeli government, as any action it took worked against its interests.   http://www.wsm.ie/c/palestine-solidarity-flotilla-gaza-riverdance-israel

13   See Human Rights Watch for a primer on this issue https://www.hrw.org/news/2014/11/21/dangerous-work-defending-transparency

14   See for example the Follow the Money campaigns https://www.one.org/international/follow-the-money/ and http://followthemoney.net/

Ideas for strategy and tactics

31. Overload the system.
This is a type of lawful 'denial of service' attack on a bureaucracy. It can also be crowd-sourced so loads of people can share in the fun. Select the activity on the basis of sensitivity and importance to the organisation. It's worth keeping in mind that while a complex letter to a bureaucracy may take you X minutes to write, it could consume X x 50 person-minutes to action at the other end.[15]

32. Act and think both local and global.
This is an important and valuable framework to adopt. Build with local communities to support and enliven a broader campaign that has state, national, regional or international effect.

33. Build an ethical framework.
This is the moral foundation that will help guide you over what could be dark and rocky roads. Don't treat your issues and actions as self-evident. By creating a moral foundation you can more easily communicate your message. And if you're going to break the law, the framework may be admissible as a defence in court – and certainly would be considered by a jury.

---

15   In the 1990's, UK campaigners against CCTV (electronic visual surveillance) urged thousands of people to lodge data protection access requests for their visual data from cameras. These actions created huge bureaucratic overload for the government authorities.

34. **Information is the new gold.** A smart activist, unless overwhelmed with current projects, will devote a set period every week to fishing around information sources. Industry and government publications, public records, parliamentary debates, court records etc. This might be targeted or speculative. The exercise is usually productive and yields data that can open up a broader landscape of interest.

35. **Be careful about making it personal.** Saul Alinsky once described one exceptional tactic as "Pick the target, freeze it, personalise it and polarise it". These days, that's a dangerous concept. Ensure that adequate thinking has been done before choosing the individual offender, along with condemning aspects such as personal circumstances – but if you do go ahead, do not lose confidence when the sympathy card is played. This is not a tactic to be undertaken lightly or without ethical consequence. Still, best to play against the role rather than against the person.

36. **Timing is the most important and least understood factor in campaigning - and often it's the only factor that matters.** Launching an initiative or releasing a report depends on at least two factors. 1) when not to launch it, for example during a major competing event or national news crisis and 2) understanding ideally when an initiative should be launched, for example during a related event in the relevant field so media outlets have a news peg to hang the story. Timing is often outside a campaigner's control, but the risk of bad timing can be reduced.

Specific campaign ideas

37. **Be funny to be noticed!** Humor, ridicule and satire are potent tactics. Comedy in any form makes you appear sane and balanced – and It is almost impossible for your opponents to counteract ridicule. In some contexts, satire is also conditionally immune from prosecution (but don't count on immunity).

38. **Use complaint processes whenever possible.** This technique is used by many groups as either forward intelligence or a fishing expedition. Whether a supermarket or a rail company, the responses (or lack of one) to complaints can indicate the sensitivity of the company and whether further action should be taken. Response data should also be collected.

39. **Where possible, create tangible or physical evidence of an assertion.** Don't just say it, do it. If you are claiming a risk or a product failure or anything that can be replicated at the physical level, test it out and have the television stations notified.[16]

---

16   In the late 1990s, privacy campaigners in the US demonstrated a hacking technique on the new US passports in front of a government official at the Computers, Freedom and Privacy conference which resulted in the passport rollout being immediately suspended.

40. Be a stakeholder manager.

One of the most useful, productive and cost effective projects you can undertake is to set up a multi-stakeholder meeting on a topical issue. If you are fighting, say, a government proposal, bring together as many affected people as possible – local shop owners, school governors, local residents, community clubs and associations etc. You'll receive kudos - and potentially build networks and coalitions.

41. Make your opponent an offer it can refuse. There's a degree of brinkmanship in this enjoyable point-scoring exercise that can be played from both sides, but is definitely worth a try. If you're in battle with an identified target, invite it to participate in a meeting that has aims that you are sure they won't agree to. Wait a few days then ask them again to a similar meeting. Two refusals looks to the public to be bloody-minded.

42. Culture Jamming is powerful and fun. Re-branding the opposition's brand is one of the most popular and potent consumer activist techniques. Unlike a single piece of satire, rebranding should be a longer-term project.[17]

43. Become a shareholder. An old tactic, but a useful one. Buy a share in your most hated company and you get an invite to the ball! Well, the AGM anyway, where you can plant questions and distribute helpfully worded material before being roughly escorted out of the building. Make sure to film every minute for posterity and evidence.

---

17 Campaigners have rebranded McDonalds to McDiabetes, Burger King to Murder King, American Idol to American Idiot and Shell to Hell http://www.hongkiat.com/blog/logo-parodies/

44.
My enemy's enemy might be my friend. Track down people who have an issue with an executive at the target organization - aggrieved business partners, court combatants, former employees. But be cautious. Those could be turbulent waters.

45.
Never underestimate the power of prayer. Yes indeed, or king and country for that matter. Rich, powerful and corrupt people often keep a foot in one religion or another. Let's see how many religious rules they break in an average week. With the right advice you might even uncover a blasphemy or a serious breach.

46.
Conduct Comparatively good research. If you want to really frustrate and anger your opponent while also inflicting real damage, produce a report which compares its customer service (or whatever) with that of its rivals. This needs to be done with care. Unless you're a well know group - or connected with a university - you'll need to confine yourself to customer-led responses.[18]

47.
The great walk-out. The action of walking away from something is powerful, particularly if you walk away "in disgust" on the basis of a sound ethical principle. Setting up a meeting then leaving it at the right moment is symbolically strong. Be careful though... that's a game two parties can play.

48.
Boycotts might not affect sales, but they can be potent. Never underestimate the potential power of a boycott. In most cases, the value of a boycott is largely symbolic, but its mere existence provides an enduring peg for media. And the beauty of a boycott is its uncompromising bluntness. Support your boycott with a foundation of evidence, liberally and very publicly distribute pamphlets, secure two or three articulate supporters and then contact local media. No-one will ever know how effective your action is in terms of product sales – and in some respects it barely matters if you have an economic impact. A boycott is a device to magnify a broader campaign.

---

18   The biggest press storm to hit Google in its then eight-year history was such a report that placed them bottom of the internet privacy league http://www.washingtonpost.com/wp-dyn/content/article/2007/06/09/AR2007060900840.html

49.
Use the party political system. Powerful people with even a mild interest in politics often have powerful enemies. Find them. Talk with them. Discover what they know.

50.
Create strange bedfellows. It's worth keeping in mind that media has a fascination for atypical collections of people. Bringing together a rare diversity of people - particularly natural enemies - into the same room creates powerful images of you being politically neutral, a facilitator or even a peace maker.[19]

19 The remarkable 1987 "people's victory" against the Australian identity card proposal was made possible in part because of an unprecedented meeting of high profile political enemies to discuss the card and then telling a wildly curious media that the meeting was secret. That gathering, together with its secret nature, provoked comment from the prime minister and drew mainstream attention to the issue   http://opennet.or.kr/wp-content/uploads/2014/05/Lessons-from-the-Australia-Card-deux-ex-machina.pdf

51. Leverage the police

The police are a free resource. Use them. Reporting a company to police under a specific part of law throws cats among the pigeons and is a strong media draw. Lodging a claim with police usually generates a crime reference number and provides media with a powerful news peg.[20]

52. Target influential people.

If you're in the business of activism, that means you have a cause. You have a cause too that other people care about, including celebrities. And as a campaigner you have a mandate to reach out to these people. People with a cause need a champion. Or a hundred champions. Write ten letters a day, twenty. TV stars, MPs, celebrities. Some will get back to you, maybe just to say they support the cause in principle. Then write to parliaments, the UN, the OECD. Names of great institutions are just as valuable. The letters you get back will be important tools that you can leverage to achieve further support.

---

20   This was achieved, for example, by UK internet privacy campaigners who filed criminal complaints against British Telecom over claims of unlawful computer intrusion. http://www.theregister.co.uk/2010/10/27/cps_bt_phorm/ This tactic was also used by Privacy International in its criminal complaint to Scotland Yard over Google's WiFi interception. https://www.theguardian.com/technology/2010/jun/22/google-wifi-crime-privacy-international

53. **What you don't know can be as important as what you know.** All serious activists at one time or another learn to turn ignorance to an advantage. In a public forum if asked any question about the company, you should respond "we don't know. We've been asking but they refuse to disclose the facts". Creating a list of questions to which there is no obvious answer is also a technique, and although a cheap shot, can have an powerful effect.

54. **Force the opponent to threaten you.** This is another one of those no-lose strategies. You'll need some legal support for the content, but tactical goading can pay off spectacularly. A basis of satire is best. This tactic is best done using physical material in a public place. Doing it online will probably result merely in a notice and takedown request to your ISP. There's limited advantage in that.

55. **Publish unanswerable technical questions.** This is a more highly evolved version of the ignorance = knowledge point above. No matter what your issue, there will be unresolved technical, scientific, health, safety, economic or legal issues. If it's a large target there will already have been debate over some of these. The tactic here is to use those points as a basis to cast doubt on others. Find new material that, no matter how thinly, connects an issue to the target, Ask questions that are actively framed: "To what extent does...", "What is the precise relationship with...", "On how many occasions have..".

56. Test the system. Investigative journalists - the few that remain at least - are fond of this strategy, Wait until a claim is made, a statistic published or an answer provided in parliament, and then road test the assertion. If, say, a statistic is published saying MPs respond to constituents letters on average in 5 days, test it and then openly contest the official figure. You can leverage the resulting interest to launch a deeper or broader campaign.

57.
Be politely troublesome. Go out of your way to be a pain. Be insistent and persistent in every interaction with your opponent, but do so in an annoyingly polite manner. Having taken a moral position on an issue, it's your duty to be a clever evangelist. You might, for example, be fighting the CEO of a retail chain, but never forget that being a constant irritant at the shop floor level will inevitably send a message up the ladder.[21]

58.
Slur by association. Check public registers to find directorship and affiliated board relationships of your opponents. Check those at the second layer to discover details of holding companies etc. Search news sites and industry publications. Look for court actions. Check public information on past employment and CV. Check out the background of each. Find negative coverage and see if a pattern can be found.

---

21 The late Neil Quigley, for example - a London motor mechanic - had been engaged in a fight with officials of Bromley Council in England over their constant intrusion over his claim for housing benefits. He made a point of printing off 30,000 word texts on human rights, into which he would randomly insert a few custom paragraphs relating to their inquiries. The authority eventually caved in.

59.

Find a victim, any victim. Media needs real people. People who are offended or angry or victimised and will stand up to a big institution. Find victims, whether friends or university mates - or in fact, anyone. Don't manufacture one though. You'll be probably be found out.

60.
Trap your opponent in a double loss position. Known as the percussion trap, this strategy envisions an initial action that triggers into a successful second response regardless of the initial outcome. This strategy is best executed when you have evidence of a company or government's wrong-doing. Choose an action such as sending a lawyer's letter that can result only in a non-response, a confirmation of wrong-doing or a denial. The letter you send initially is non-specific and effectively entraps the target by creating an irresistible urge to deny. If however a confirmation is sent, it can be published as a success for you, and can then be forwarded to a regulatory authority, lawyer or media for second phase action. A denial can be followed up with an attack for deception and lying, again with a legal or media follow-up. A refusal to answer makes the company appear guilty - and can be kept as an open case on your website or elsewhere.

Negatives to positives

61.
Plan for a victorious defeat. This is a very important process in the long view of campaigning, which envisions future repeat engagement. Political candidates are familiar with a variation on this theme. A member of Parliament may lose a seat at an election but if a come-back is anticipated the farewell speech will be gracious and empowered.

62. Always respond to an accusation of inaccuracy with a counterclaim of secrecy.
Corporations routinely accuse campaigners of making false statements. If you get the opportunity, respond aggressively with an assertion that your assessment is a direct result of their own obfuscation and deception.

63. Turn adverse public opinion to your advantage.
Opinion polling often works against the interests of campaigners, but this doesn't have to be the case. Elected officials are keen on making such statements as "I haven't received one single letter about this issue', which should invite the response "well that just proves what an appalling job the government has done in educating people about the risks".

Painting by the Voina group on a bascule bridge in front of the FSB headquarter in St Petersburg.

Critical campaign risk factors and risk mitigation

64. Understand the elastic limit of your supporters. Alinsky describes this rule as "Never go outside the experience of your people", but there's more to it than that. Campaign leaders should always recognise that their own motivation and rewards are not shared equally by all supporters. In a rush to achieve greater progress through new avenues, leaders can easily leave their supporters behind. This has been the unfortunate fate of countless campaigns.

65. Don't risk staking everything on media coverage. Media are notoriously fickle on most subjects in terms of what they will cover. Media organisations are subject to numerous variables and any commitments should be treated skeptically, even if the journalist is known to you. Do not make the success of your activities dependent on coverage.

66. Keep your messaging consistent and real. Campaigns that don't carefully manage their messaging will drift from inconsistency to contradiction before swerving into fatal hypocrisy. Find a good slogan and stick to it.

67. **Never concede or confess anything to the opponent.** While you're in the campaign phase, whether in public or in private, on or off the record, never concede anything until such point as you're ready to negotiate formally. Treat a combatant in a campaign like a police officer who has arrested you. You may be lulled into revealing or conceding something, but the general advice is never to do so. In terms of public statements, never give praise unless it is tightly defined (say in a press statement) and never be bullied or seduced into admitting you were wrong.

68. **Negative campaigns should imagine a constructive alternative.** This isn't the same as saying that it's an activist's responsibility to find alternatives to the schemes they fight, but it's always a useful strategy to have an alternative in your back pocket - even if you don't elaborate on the detail. Describing safer and better alternative approaches also presents an appearance that you are knowledgeable and constructive. Creatively visualise what that constructive alternative might be. At the very least it's an insurance policy against hostile media.

Media and Communications strategy

69. If your issue can't be expressed in a nine-word headline, you have a thesis, not a campaign. As an activist striving to win hearts and minds, you're competing with thousands of other pressing issues – many of them fueled by richly resourced backers. Imagine a tightly compressed 'elevator pitch' in which you have three seconds to grab people's attention. The didactic stuff can follow from that. It's not intellectually dishonest to win over a potential audience with a captivating teaser, and it's a substantially better approach than explaining your position by starting with "OK, give me five minutes and I'll tell you why this is important".

70. A successful first strike in media offers opportunity to the opponent. Never confuse a first strike with a tactical advantage. Opening up an issue to the media provides your opponent with an opportunity to retaliate, perhaps by asserting that your "misguided" position is precisely why the particular initiative was undertaken in the first place. A first strike usually has overwhelming value if it is shocking, rather than merely challenging or reportive.

ways ideas ntrepreneur
building today
brand white keys
help good
smm
successful strategy
tips essentials 10 best
field campaign likes business need start
old read tweets creating effective
free report
guide create time government develop
https solutions hootsuite gain
success
socialmedia 2014
paper steps
seo

71. A good media strategy ensures you'll always be quoted, but a great media strategy hands you the headline. It's easy to be happy with being the dingleberry at the end of a news story – the responding quote stuck at the end of a story – but the true science of media moves this responsive add-on into the thrust of the piece. This requires quick thinking before you speak to a journalist. Threaten an action, launch an initiative, send a letter, start a petition. Any action you take has a good chance of stealing the first paragraph of the story, if not the headline.

72. **Use active language and don't be afraid to speak your mind.** Passive and conciliatory words like "worried" or "concerned" do little to advance your cause and serve only to confuse the public. They are just one step removed from diplomatic shockers like "regret" and "unfortunate". Media love real people with real emotions. Be cautiously angry. Be constructively furious. Be logically incandescent with rage about an issue – and temper this emotion with evidence and reason.

73. **Take back the language.** Corporations, in particular, have made a science of manipulating language. Listen carefully to the exact way PR people try to soften or neutralise words, then push those words back where they rightfully belong. Replace the opponent's words with your own, and evangelise for others to do the same.

74. **Symbols can be more powerful than words.** A symbol – if ingeniously designed – can become a shorthand expression for your entire cause. It becomes both an endorsement and a rallying cry. Creating a symbol – like a logo – also gives an appearance of solidity and substance.

75. Images can be more potent than text. Photographs take up a large (and often fixed) proportion of any news publication and yet few campaigners exploit that resource. Look for innovative opportunities, take your own royalty-free pics and - corny as it sounds - always consider the cliche of children, animals and bizarre scenarios, making a guaranteed photo opp success.

Gerald Holtom made this first draft of a symbol to be used in a three day march from London to the weapons research establishment at Aldermaston in 1958. One of the organisers was Michael Randle who recalls a veteran peace campaigner coming up to him shortly after the first leaflet bearing the motif had been printed to complain that he and the others must have been out of their minds for adopting it - it would never catch on!

76. You are what you write. A campaign can live or die on the clarity of its writing. Find someone who is genuinely artistic - and treat that writer as a core team member.

77. Get real about the value of media coverage. Don't get mesmerised by a mention in the media. As a rule of thumb, aim at a hundred mentions to get on the radar screen and a thousand mentions to start shifting public opinion.

78. Viral a credible conspiracy. Everyone loves a conspiracy, so start one. Some of the most powerful attack-virals on YouTube are those that drew connections between Facebook's directors and a string of arms companies and national security agencies. In reality those sort of connections can be drawn with most major companies, but the tactic had its intended impact. Be creative, but base your conspiracy on evidence.

79. Do all the running for media. The more preparation you do, the greater the chance you'll be covered. Include quotes, good pics, the contact number of an independent expert. High quality graphics guarantee consideration of a feature placement.

80. Make your website more than a soap box. It's not just a place you hang your manifesto, but a place to generate ideas and controversy. Make it a resource centre to recruit new supporters in a practical way.

Guiding principles for campaign planning and formation

81. Strategically brand your public identity. Imagine from the beginning, the characteristics that you feel best represent your group and its ethos, then seek broad feedback on the name and other prominent imagery. Branding is not just name and colours, it is the feel - internally and externally - of everything the organization represents.

82. A good tactic is one your supporters enjoy. This outcome requires a mix of sensitivity and dialogue to ensure that people know in advance the options that they want to pursue. Empower them with choice if at all possible.

83. Become academic. Universities and colleges are finally starting to open up to the real world, even at the community and advocacy level (in some parts of Europe they call this 'policy engagement'). Indeed in some countries their funding depends on it. Make inroads into an institution and slowly build the relationship.

84. Always ensure your campaign lifespan is sustainable.
This element is dependent on the motivation of staff and should be reviewed regularly. If your campaign drags on too long without evolution, the support base is likely to fall away. If necessary, re-structure your campaign.

85. Create partnerships to empower the campaign. At the earliest stage, brainstorm to identify the range of organisations related to your area. Figure out what you can offer them, whether they are likely to work with you and at what likely level. Conduct background research and then seek initial scoping meetings, rather than asking up front for a yes or no. Build the relationship.

Critical risk factors for the campaign organization

86. Avoid the hothouse. During the early stages of activity - in which most of the framework for a campaign will be formed - it's always good advice to be particularly conscious that single-issue activists working in a hothouse environment can spark a condition of suspended reality. In this situation, strength of passion can override mature judgment and can often be blind to contrary evidence and risk. At an early stage, devise a conflict resolution framework.

87.
There is no single formula for a decision structure. Different campaign environments call for different approaches to how decisions are made. Democratising a campaign might be essential, but it can also lead to dangerous waters. It's tempting to presume that any campaign for rights or freedoms must have a democratic structure. And while this is theoretically true, a vast number of campaigns fall apart because of a failure of timing. In practical terms, leadership trumps democracy in the early stages of most actions. There's an interesting division of views on this topic, with some campaigners believing that actions should arise from a democratic environment and others who believe that democracy can be an artificial imposition on a functioning campaign infrastructure. Whether you democratise or not, expect this debate to emerge.

88. Maintain humility in leadership. One of the most common campaign failures is when leaders allow their ego to trump the needs of the campaign itself. The cult of personality can be a powerful tool for campaigns, but this approach also invites vulnerability.

89. Protect the organisation from castration. Never put all your eggs into the one basket. Resources or financial support that has been quickly acquired can just as quickly be lost. Create diversity in all areas of your activity – particularly funding.

90. When planning a campaign, never assume continued support from any quarter unless you've considered all possible circumstances for its withdrawal. Countless campaigns have fallen into the trap of assuming that supporters – particularly supporters from the political and corporate worlds – will indefinitely embrace their issue. This is historically not the case. Large organisations and political entities are fickle and are prone to reversing their support if even the slightest element of the issue starts to shift. Others may bail at the first sign of controversy.

91. No matter how highly you rate your value as a campaigner, your symbolic worth is greater to the opponent. Be wary of being captured by getting too close to your opponent or inadvertently endorsing it through participation or association.

92. Take full risk and contingency measures to protect your infrastructure. A scan needs to be made from time to time of risk factors in you org. How to mitigate chances of failure, whether survival depends on a single staffer and whether enough progress is being made for sustainability. In high risk situations, look to any weakness in your personal life, and also those of other staff. Ensure that guidelines have been followed. Be aware that success also brings opportunities for attack – internally and externally. With this knowledge, mitigation measures can be taken. Imagine disaster scenarios and create contingency plans. Run a risk brainstorm every so often to identify the elements of your campaign infrastructure that are critical to its success (whether that's an individual, an IT system or funding), then establish an emergency plan to deal with calamity.

Guiding principles for managing and sustaining a campaign infrastructure

93. Keep the pressure on. Use various tactics and actions and make leaders responsible for finding and supporting team-led initiatives.

94. Do something surprising. Most beneficial of all, surprise yourselves. Set a target to take an action every so often and challenge yourselves to come up with a radical initiative. This will energise you and break stereotypes. You may even find new activist avenues in the process.

95. Know the difference between keep control letting go of control.

No successful major campaign in the history of human rights has ever managed to keep central control of the issue. Once a campaign has become a truly national issue a thousand uncontrolled strands will emerge from the ground. Any attempt to control this dynamic would be fruitless and even fatal. Campaigners should be aware that one consequence of success will be the forfeiture of control.[22]

---

22   For an example of the mechanics of a successful decentralised campaign, see the ACTA analysis at http://techpresident.com/news/22311/germany-activists-help-coordinate-europe-wide-anti-acta-protests

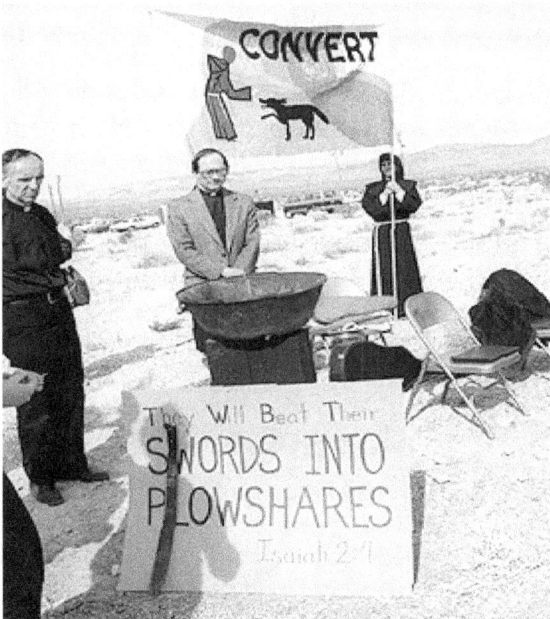

96. **Create a project-resource program.** This activity supports structural sustainability and organically builds resources. Actively seek out volunteers who are good at digging up anything from paper supplies to free office space. Aim to secure at least one new resource item each day. Within a few weeks this investment will pay off to a sometimes critically important extent.

97. **Love your team.** If you're the leader of a team, particularly a small team, treat it as if it were a partnership. Care for it, nurture it, spend time with it, but always remember that with no notice it might take on a life of its own. This shouldn't make you a hardened cynic, merely an informed leader who wears protective clothing. In a stressed and tight ecosystem many actions and words can be misinterpreted, leading to a sense of betrayal. The reality is that most small campaigning groups, like most rock bands, implode through stress or relationship issues, While being the most precious element of an organisation they can, without care, be its most dangerous threat. Make them feel needed, never take them for granted, don't act like god - and in victory, give them the credit.

98. **Do conventionally good things.** There are a few solid reasons behind this idea, particularly if you're an activist who doesn't like the stereotype. It's always sound policy to do nice things beyond activism. This isn't so much digging flower beds, but sending congratulation emails or letters to people who you noticed doing something useful or praiseworthy. Academics who write a good paper, journalists who run a great story and so on. Your contact list and your reputation can only benefit. Give them praise. And be the change that you want to see!

99. **Know your technology.** IT and comms systems are critically important tools for many activists. The technology is also useful to government as a means of finding out what you're up to, so protect yourselves and don't needlessly give away your tactics. It's crucial to learn not just what IT gear can do for your operations, but how to use encryption and circumvention techniques to avoid scrutiny. Brief supporters regularly. Help them protect themselves.

100. **Lighten up!** Following on from the principle of team building it's important to equip yourself with a virtual "frownometer" to check how joyless you've all become. Many activist groups fall to pieces because being involved is just too painful. Do fun things. Do Fun Actions - and celebrate regularly. It is your duty to be optimistic!

Other resources for activists

www.nonviolence.wri-irg.org/en

www.bmartin.cc/pubs/08gm.html

www.umass.edu/resistancestudies

www.bmartin.cc/pubs/backfire.html

www.beautifultrouble.org

www.blueprintforrevolution.com

www.canvasopedia.org

www.resistance-journal.org

www.civilresistance.info

www.civilengagement.org

www.nonviolent-conflict.org

www.facebook.com/stellan.vinthagen

www.aeinstein.org

www.organizingforpower.org

www.newtactics.org

www.riverasun.com/workshops

www.nvdatabase.swarthmore.edu

https://tosdr.org

www.ingramcontent.com/pod-product-compliance
Lightning Source LLC
LaVergne TN
LVHW051710080426
835511LV00017B/2828